ADDRESS

BEFORE THE

PHI BETA KAPPA

AT

YALE COLLEGE,

July 26, 1854.

BY

WILLIAM H. SEWARD.

NEW HAVEN:
PRINTED BY B. L. HAMLEN,
Printer to Yale College.
1854.

New Haven, July 26, 1854.

Hon. William H. Seward:

Dear Sir—We are directed by a vote of the Phi Beta Kappa Society, Yale College, to thank you for the luminous and profound Discourse delivered by you before the Society this evening, and to request in behalf of the Society a copy for publication.

With great regard, we are very respectfully yours,

A. N. Skinner,
Horace Bushnell,
Henry Dutton,
Committee.

Washington, July 29, 1854.

Gentlemen—I send herewith, a copy of the Address to which you have so kindly referred, and have the honor to be, very respectfully,

Your humble servant,

William H. Seward.

Messrs. *A. N. Skinner*, *Horace Bushnell*, and *Henry Dutton*, Committee, &c. &c., New Haven.

ADDRESS.

Gentlemen:

A political discourse may seem out of time and out of place at a classic festival and in academic groves. Nevertheless, the office of instructor to a prince brought something more of dignity even to the learning and piety of Fenelon. To study the forces and tendency of a Republic which is not obscure, cannot, therefore, at any time or in any place, be unbecoming an association which regards universal philosophy as the proper guide of human life.

Nations are intelligent, moral persons, existing for the ends of their own happiness and the improvement of mankind. They grow, mature, and decline. Their physical development, being most obvious, always attracts our attention first. Certainly we cannot too well understand the material condition of our own country. "I think," said Burke, sadly, addressing the British House of Commons, just after the American war, "I think I can trace all the calamities of this country to the single source of not having had steadily before our eyes a general, comprehensive, well-connected, and well-proportioned view of the whole of our dominions, and a just sense of their bearings and relations."

Trace on a map the early boundaries of the United States, as they were defined by the treaty of Versailles, in 1783. See with what jealousy Great Britain abridged their enjoyment of the fisheries on the Northeast coast, and how tenaciously she locked up against them the St. Lawrence, the only possible channel between their inland regions and the Atlantic ocean. Observe how Spain, while retaining the vast and varied solitudes which spread out westward from the Mississippi river to the Pacific ocean, at the same time assigned the thirty-first parallel of north latitude as the southern boundary of the United States, and thus shut them out from access by that river or otherwise to the Gulf of Mexico. See now how the massive and unpassable Alleghany Mountains traversed the new Republic from north to south, dividing it into two regions—the inner one rich in agricultural resources, but without markets; and the outer one adapted to defence and markets, but wanting the materials for commerce. Were not the Europeans astute in thus confining the United States within limits which would probably render an early separation of them inevitable, and would also prevent equally the whole and each of the future parts from ever becoming a formidable or even a really independent Atlantic power? They had cause for their jealousies. They were monarchies, and they largely divided the western hemisphere between them. The United States aimed to become a maritime nation, and their success would tend to make that hemisphere not only republican, but also independent of Europe. That success was foreseen. A British statesman, in describing the American Colonies just before the peace, had said to his countrymen: "Your children do not grow faster from infancy to manhood than they spread from families to communities, and from villages to nations."

The United States, thus confined landward, betook themselves to the sea, whose broad realm lay unappropriated; and, having furnished themselves with shipping and seamen equal to the adventurous pursuit of the whale fishery under the Poles, they presented themselves in European ports as a maritime people. Afterwards, their well-known attitude of neutrality, in a season of general war, enabled them to become carriers for the world. But they never forgot for a moment the importance of improving their position on the coast. France was now the owner of the Province of Louisiana, which stretched all along the western bank of the Mississippi. She wisely sold a possession, which she was unable to defend, to the United States, who thus, only twenty years after the treaty of Versailles, secured the exclusive navigation of the great river; and, descending from their inland frontier, established themselves on the coast of the Gulf of Mexico. Spain soon saw that her colonies on that coast, east of the Mississippi, now virtually surrounded by the United States, were untenable. She therefore, for an equivalent, ceded the Floridas, and retired behind the Sabine; and so the sea coast of the United States was now seen to begin at that river, and passing along the Gulf and around the Peninsula, and beyond the Capes, to terminate at the St. Croix, in the Bay of Fundy.

The course of the European war showed that Spain was exhausted. Nearly all her American Colonies, inspired by the example of the United States, and sustained by their sympathy, struck for independence, established Republican systems, and entered into treaties of amity and commerce with the Republic of the North.

But the United States yet needed a northern passage from their western valleys to the Atlantic ocean. The new channel to be opened must necessarily have connections, natural or artificial, with the inland rivers and lakes. An internal trade ramifying the country was a necessary basis for commerce, and it would constitute the firmest possible national union. Practically, there was in the country neither a canal to serve for a model, nor an engineer competent to project one. The railroad invention had not yet been perfected in Europe, nor even conceived in the United States. The Federal Government alone had adequate resources, but, after long consideration and some unprofitable experiments, it not only disavowed the policy, but also disclaimed the power of making internal improvements. Private capital was unavailable for great national enterprises.

The States were not convinced of the wisdom of undertaking singly works within their own borders which would be wholly or in part useless, unless extended beyond them by other States, and which, even although they should be useful to themselves, would be equally or more beneficial to States which refused or neglected to join in their construction. Moreover, the only source of revenue in the States was direct taxation—always unreliable in a popular Government—and they had no established credits, at home or abroad. Nevertheless, the people comprehended the exigency, and their will opened a way through all these embarrassments. The State of New York began, and she has hitherto, although sometimes faltering, prosecuted this great enterprise with unsurpassed fidelity. The other States, according to their respective abilities and convictions of interest and duty, have coöperated. By canals we have extended the navigation of Chesapeake bay to the coal-fields of Maryland at Cumberland, and also by the way of Columbia to the coal-fields of Pennsylvania. By canals we have united Chesapeake bay with the Delaware river, and have, with alternating railroads, connected that river with the Ohio river and with Lake Erie. By canals we have opened a navigation between Philadelphia and New York, mingling the waters of the Delaware with those of the Raritan. By canals we have given access from two several ports on the Hudson to two different coal-fields in Pennsylvania. By canals we have also extended the navigation of the Hudson through Lake Champlain and its outlet, to the St. Lawrence near Montreal. We are just opening a channel from the Hudson to Cape Vincent, on Lake Ontario, near its eastern termination, while we long since have opened one from the same river to a central harbor on that lake at Oswego. A corresponding improvement, made by the Canadian authorities on the opposite shore, prolongs our navigation from Lake Ontario to Lake Erie. We have also connected the Hudson river with the eastern branch of the Susquehanna, through the valley of the Chenango, and again with its western tributaries through the Seneca Lake. We are also uniting the Hudson with the Alleghany, a tributary of the Mississippi, through the valley of the Genesee. One long trunk of canal receives the trade gathered by most of these tributary channels, while it directly unites the Hudson with Lake Erie at Buffalo. The shores of that great lake are the basis of a second part of the same system. Canals connect the Alleghany, in the State of Pennsylvania, with Lake Erie at Erie; the Ohio river, at Portage and at Cincinnati, with Lake Erie, at Cleveland and Toledo; and again the Ohio river, in the State of Indiana, with Lake Erie, through the valley of the Wabash. Lake Superior, hitherto secluded from even internal commerce, is now being connected with the other great lakes by the canal of the Falls of St. Mary; and, to complete the whole, the Illinois canal unites the lakes and all the extensive system I have described, with the Mississippi. Thus, by substituting works purely artificial, we have not only dispensed with the navigation of the St. Lawrence, but have also opened a complete circuit of inland navigation and traffic between New Orleans, on the Gulf, and New York, Philadelphia, and Baltimore, on the Atlantic. The aggregate length of those canals is five thousand miles, and that of the inland coasts thus washed by natural and artificial channels exceeds twenty thousand miles.

Railroads constitute an auxiliary system of improvements, at once more complex and more comprehensive. By railroads we have connected, or are in the act of connecting, together all the principal seaports on the Atlantic coast and on the coasts of the Gulf of Mexico, namely: Portland, Boston, New York, Philadelphia, Baltimore, Norfolk, Charleston, Mobile, and New Orleans. Again—railroads from each or most of these ports proceed inland through important towns, to great dépôts on the St. Lawrence, the Lakes, the Ohio, and the Mississippi, namely: Quebec, Montreal, Ogdensburgh, Oswego, Rochester, Buffalo, Erie, Cleveland, Sandusky, Toledo, Monroe, Detroit, Chicago, Pittsburgh, Cincinnati, Louisville, St. Louis, Cairo, and Memphis. Again —there are tributaries which search out agricultural and mineral productions and fabrics, accumulated at less notable points; and so a complete system is perfected, which leaves no inhabited region unexplored, while it has for its base the long line of seaboard. The aggregate length of these railroads is sixteen thousand miles, and the total cost is six hundred millions of dollars.

Immediately after the purchase of Louisiana, President Jefferson having conceived the idea of a national establishment on the Pacific coast, an exploration of the intervening wastes was made. An American navigator about the same time visited the coast itself, and thus laid the foundation of a title by discovery. A commercial settlement, afterwards planted on the Columbia river by the late John Jacob Astor, perished in the war of 1812. Ten years ago, the great thought of Pacific colonization revived, under the influence of the commercial activity resulting from the successful progress of the system of Internal Improvements. Oregon was settled. Two years afterwards, its boundaries were defined, and it was politically organized; and now it constitutes two prosperous Territories.

The social, military, and ecclesiastical institutions of Mexico, proved unfavorable to an immediate success of the Republican system. Revolution became a chronic disease there. Texas separated, and practically became independent, although Mexico refused to recognize her separation. After some years, Texas was admitted as a State into our Federal Union. A war which ensued, resulted not only in the relinquishment of Mexican claims upon Texas, but in the extension of her coast frontier to the Rio Grande, and also in the annexation of New Mexico and Upper California to the United States.

Thus, in sixty-five years after the peace of Versailles, the United States advanced from the Mississippi, and occupied a line stretching through eighteen degrees of latitude on the Pacific coast, overlooking the Sandwich Islands and Japan, and confronting China, (the Cathay for which Columbus was in search when he encountered the bewildering vision of San Domingo.) The new possession was divided into two Territories and the State of California. The simultaneous discovery of native gold in the sands and rocks of that State resulted in the instantaneous establishment of an active commerce, not only with our Atlantic cities, but also with the ports of South America and with the maritime countries of Europe, with the Sandwich Islands, and even with China. Thus the United States ceased to be a mere Atlantic Nation, and assumed the attitude of a great Continental Power, enjoying ocean navigation on either side, and bearing equal and similar relations to the eastern and to the western coast of the old world. The national connections between the Atlantic and Pacific regions are yet incomplete; but the same spirit which has brought them into political union is at work still, and no matter what the Government may do or may leave undone, the necessary routes of commerce, altogether within and across our own domain, will be established.

The number of States has increased since this aggrandizement began, from seventeen to thirty-one; the population from five millions to twenty-four millions; the tonnage employed in commerce from one million to four and a half millions; and the National revenue from ten millions to sixty millions of dollars. Within that period, Spain has retired altogether from the Continent, and two considerable islands in the Antilles are all that remains of the New World, which, hardly four centuries ago, the generous and pious Genoese navigator, under the patronage of Isabella, gave to the Kingdoms of Castile and Leon. Great Britain tenders us now the freedom of the fisheries and of the St.

Lawrence, on conditions of favor to the commerce of her Colonies, and even deliberates on the policy of releasing them from their allegiance. The influences of the United States on the American continent have resulted already in the establishment of the Republican system everywhere, except in Brazil, and even there, in limiting Imperial power. In Europe, they have awakened a war of opinion, that, after spreading desolation into the steppes of Russia, and to the base of the Carpathian Mountains, has only been suppressed for a time by combination of the capital and of the political forces of that continent. In Africa, those influences, aided by the benevolent efforts of our citizens, have produced the establishment of a Republic, which, beginning with the abolition of the traffic in slaves, is going steadily on towards the moral regeneration of its savage races. In the Sandwich Islands, those influences have already effected, not only such a regeneration of the natives, but also a political organization, which is bringing that important commercial station directly under our protection. Those influences have opened the ports of Japan, and secured an intercourse of commerce and friendship with its extraordinary people—numbering forty millions—thus overcoming a policy of isolation which they had practised for an hundred and fifty years. The same influences have not only procured for us access to the five principal ports of China, but also have generated a revolution there, which promises to bring the three hundred millions living within that vast empire into the society of the western nations.

How magnificent is the scene which the rising curtain discloses to us here! and how sublime the pacific part assigned to us!

> "The Eastern nations sink, their glory ends,
> And Empire rises where the sun descends."

But, restraining the imagination from its desire to follow the influences of the United States in their future progress through the Manillas, and along the Indian coast, and beyond the Persian Gulf, to the far-off Mozambique, let us dwell for a moment on the visible results of the national aggrandizement at home. Wealth has everywhere increased, and has been equalized with much success in all the States, new as well as old. Industry has persevered in opening newly discovered resources, and bringing forth their treasures, as well as in the establishment of the productive arts. The Capitol, which at first seemed too pretentious, is extending itself northward and southward upon its noble terrace, to receive the representatives of new incoming States. The departments of Executive administration continually expand under their lofty arches and behind their lengthening colonades. The Federal city so recently ridiculed for its ambitious solitudes, is extending its broad avenues in all directions, and, under the hands of native artists, is taking on the graces, as well as the fullness, of a capital. Where else will you find authority so august as in a Council composed of the Representatives of thirty States, attended by embassadors from every free city, every republic, and every court, in the civilized world? In near proximity and in intimate connection with that capital, a metropolis has arisen, which gathers, by the agency of canals, of railroads, and of coastwise navigation, the products of industry in every form throughout the North American States, as well those under foreign jurisdiction as those which constitute the Union, and distributes them in exchange over the globe; a city whose wealth and credit supply or procure the capital employed in all the great financial movements within the Republic, and whose press, in all its departments of science, literature, religion, philanthropy, and politics, is a national one. Thus expansion and aggrandizement, whose natural tendency is to produce debility and dissolution, have operated here to create, what before was wanting, a social, political, and commercial centre.

In considering the causes of this material growth, allowance must be made, liberally made for great advantages of space, climate, and resources, as well as for the weakness of outward resistance, for the vices of foreign Governments, and for the disturbed and painful condition of society under them—causes which have created and sustained a tide of emigration towards the United States unparalleled, at least, in modern times. But when all this allowance shall have been made, we shall still find that the phenomena is chiefly due to the operation here of some great ideas, either unknown before, or not before rendered so effective. These ideas are, first, the equality of men in a State, that is to say, the equality of men constituting a State; secondly, the equality of States in a combination, or, in other words, the equality of States constituting a nation. By the Constitution of every State in the American Union, each citizen is guarantied his natural rights of life, liberty, and the pursuit of happiness; and he, at the same time, is guarantied a share of the sovereign power, equal to that which can be assumed by any other citizen. This is the equality of men in the State. By the Constitution of the United States, there are no subjects. Every citizen of any one State is a free and equal citizen of the United States. Again, by the Constitution of the United States, there are no permanent provinces, or dependencies. The Union is constituted by States, and all of them stand upon the same level of political rights. This is the equality of States in the Nation.

The reduction of the two abstractions which I have mentioned into the concrete, in the Constitution of the United States, was like most other inventions, mainly due to accident. There were thirteen several States, in each of which, owing to fortunate circumstances attending their original colonization, each citizen was not only free, but also practically equal in his exercise of political power to every other citizen of that State. The freedom and equality of the citizen, and the inalienability of his natural rights were solemnly reaffirmed in the Declaration of Independence. These thirteen States were severally free and independent of each other. They therefore were equal States. Each was a sovereign. They needed free and mutual commerce among themselves, and some regulations for securing to each equal facilities of commerce with foreign countries. A union was necessary to the attainment of these ends. But the citizens of each State were unwilling to surrender either their natural and inalienable rights, *or the guardianship* of them, to a common Government over them all, even to attain the union which they needed so much. So a Federal Central Government was established, which was sovereign only in commerce, at home and abroad, and in the necessary communications with other nations; that is to say, sovereign only in regard to the mutual internal relations of the States themselves, and in regard to foreign affairs. In this Government the States are practically equal constituents, although the equality was modified by some limitations found necessary to secure the assent of some of the States. The States were not dissolved, nor disorganized, but they remained really States, just as before, existing independently of each other and of the Union, and exercising sovereignty in all the municipal departments of society. The citizen of each State also retained all his natural rights equally in the Union and in the State to which he belonged, and the United States were constituted by the whole mass of such citizens throughout all the several States. There was an unoccupied common domain, which the several States surrendered to the Federal authorities, to the end that it might be settled, colonized, and divided into other States, to be organized and to become members of the Union on an equal footing with the original States. When additions to this domain were made from foreign countries, the same principles seemed to be the only ones upon which the Government could be extended over them, and so, with some qualifications unimportant on the present occasion, they became universal in their application.

No other nation, pursuing a career of aggrandizement, has adopted the great ideas thus developed in the United States. The Macedonian conquered kingdoms for the mere gratification of conquest, and they threw off the sway he established over them as soon as the sword dropped from his hand. The Romans conquered, because the alien was a barbarian rival and enemy, and because Rome must fill the world alone. The empire, thus extended, fell under the blows of enemies, subjugated but not subdued, as soon as the central power had lost its vigor. The Ottoman, although he conquered with the sword, conciliated the subjected tribes by admitting them to the rites of a new and attractive religion. The religion, however, was of this world, and sensual, and therefore it debased its votaries. France attempted to conquer Europe in retaliation for wrongs committed against herself; but the bow broke in her hands, just as it was bent to discharge the last shaft. Spain has planted many Colonies and conquered many States, but the Castillian was proud and haughty; he enslaved the native and oppressed the creole. The Czar wins his way amid kindred races, as a parent extending protection in the enjoyment of a common religion. But the paternal relation in politics is a fiction of despotism, which extinguishes all individual energy and all social ambition. Great Britain has been distinguished from all these vulgar conquerors. She is a civilizer and a missionary. She has planted many Colonies in the West, and conquered many and vast countries in the East, and has carried English laws and the English language around the world. But Great Britain at home is an aristocracy. Her Colonies can neither be equal to her, nor yet independent. Her subjects in those countries may be free, but they cannot be Britons. Consequently, her dependencies are always discontented, and insomuch as they are possessed or swayed by freemen, they are only retained in their connection with the British throne by the presence of military and naval force. You identify an American

State or Colony by the absence of the Federal power. Everywhere, on the contrary, you identify a British Colony, whether in British America, or on the Pacific coast, or on its islands, or in Bombay, and or at St. Helena, or at Gibraltar, or on the Ionian isles, by the music of the imperial drum-beat and the frown of royal battlements. Great Britain always inspires fear, and often commands respect, but she has no friends in the wide family of nations. So it has happened, that heretofore nations have either repelled, or exhausted, or disgusted the Colonies they planted and the countries they conquered.

The United States, on the contrary, expand by force, not of arms, but of attraction. The native colonist no sooner reaches a new and distant home, whether in a cleft of the Rocky Mountains or on the seashore, than he proceeds to found a State, in which his natural and inalienable rights shall be secure, and which shall become an equal member of the Federal Union, enjoying its protection, and sharing its growing greatness and renown. Adjacent States, though of foreign habits, religion, and descent, especially if they are defenceless, look with favor upon the approach of a power that will leave them in full enjoyment of the rights of nature, and, at the same time that it may absorb them, will spare their corporate existence and individuality. The attraction increases as commerce widens the circle of the national influence.

If these positions seem to require qualification at all, the very modifications will nevertheless, serve to illustrate and sustain, the general principles involved. The people of Mexico resist annexation because they fear it would result in their being outnumbered by Americans, and so lead to the restoration of African slavery, which they have abolished. The natives of the Sandwich Islands take alarm lest by annexation they may themselves be reduced to slavery. The people of the Canadas hesitate because they disapprove the modification of the principles of equality of men and of States in favor of slaveholding States, which were admitted in the Federal Constitution.

What is the moral to be drawn from the physical progress of the United States? It is, that the strongest bonds of cohesion in society are commerce and gratitude for protected freedom.

While the majestic physical progress of the United States is no longer denied as a fact, it is, nevertheless, too generally regarded as purely accidental, and likely to cease through a want of corresponding intelligence and virtue. The principle assumed in this reasoning is just. A nation deficient in intelligence and virtue is an ignoble one, and no ignoble race can enlarge or even retain empire. But examination will show that the facts assumed are altogether erroneous. In order to prove that we are deficient in intelligence, the monuments of ancient and modern nations, all of whom have either completed their courses or passed the middle point, are arrayed before us, and we are challenged to exhibit similar monuments of equal merit on the part of the United States; as if time was not an essential condition of achievement, and as if, also, circumstances exerted no influence in directing the activity of nations. It is true that we can show no campaigns equal to those of Cæsar, or of Frederick, or of Napoleon; and no inspirations of the divine art equal to the Iliad, or the Eneid, or the Inferno, or the dramas of Shakspeare. But it is equally true, that neither Greece, nor Rome, nor France, nor England, has erected a tower as high as Babel, or a mausoleum so massive as the grand Pyramid.

Reasoning *à priori*, it is manifest, that insomuch as the physical progress of the United States has been unprecedented while it has followed a method, and insomuch as this progress has been conducted with magnanimity through many temptations and embarrassments, it is of itself no unworthy monument of national intelligence.

The Constitutions (of the States and of the Union) are confessedly unsurpassed. Grant, as is true, that all the great political ideas which are embodied in them, were before known; grant, moreover, that a favorable conjuncture for reducing those abstractions to the concrete had come; grant, also, that favorable conditions of nature and human society concurred—nevertheless, even then was ever higher genius, or greater talent, displayed, in conducting the affairs of men, than were exercised first in framing the many peculiar and delicate parts of that system of Government, with proportions so accurate that each might bear the very tension and pressure to which it was to be exposed, and then in bringing all those parts together, and forging them into one great machine with such wonderful skill, that at the very first touch of the propelling popular spring, it went at once into full and perfect operation, and has continued its movements for seventy years, in prosperity as well as in adversity, amid the factions generated by a long peace, and the disturbances of war—not only without interruption or irregularity, but even without a jar. Consider the sagacity of the people that, amid the clouds of jealousy and the storms of passion, raised by heated partisans, deliberately examined, and resolutely adopted, that wonderful yet untried mechanism, so contrived for their use, and decided that it should not merely have a trial, but should stand forever, the only Government of themselves and of their posterity. Consider, that not only was this vast engine set in motion by the voluntary act of the people, but it has also been kept in motion by their own perpetually renewed consent and direct activity; and that, although like every other combination of forces, it has its dead points, yet it passes through them with perfect regularity, and without even any sensible diminution of motion, owing to the watchful performance by the people at critical moments, of the functions devolved upon them. Consider how many and various are the human wills, which meet and concur every time a fresh impulse is given to the great mechanism. A majority of the States, neglecting or refusing to act on any such occasion, could bring the Government to a dead stand. Consider that the people not only interfere on such critical occasions, but also that they are continually supplying the necessary force to sustain the movements of the subordinate parts of the machine.

There are two and a half millions of electors, and every one of these is charged with the performance, for the most part annually, of four classes of functions, in as many distinct spheres. Once, generally in each year, the electors choose a mayor or supervisor, aldermen or trustees, or selectmen, justices of the peace, police officers, clerks, assessors of taxes, commissioners of public charities, commissioners of streets, roads, and bridges, and subalterns, or other officers of the militia, in their respective cities, towns, or other forms of municipalities. Again—the electors, generally once in each year, choose officers nearly as numerous, and of a higher grade, to execute, judicial, ministerial, and fiscal powers, of a similar nature, within the counties, which embrace several cities, towns, and municipalities. Again—they elect Governors, Lieutenant Governors, Senators and Representatives, Judges, Treasurers, and Ministers of Finance, of Education, of Public Works and of Charities, in the States constituted by such counties—States sovereign in all things, except the few departments they have voluntarily assigned to the Federal Union. Once more—the citizens choose, once in two years, Representatives, and once in three years, Senators, who exercise the legislative powers of the Republic; and once in four years, the Vice President and President of the United States, its Chief Executive Magistrates. The peace, order, prosperity, and happiness, and even the safety of society, rest manifestly on the soundness of judgment with which these many and various electoral trusts are discharged. Reflect, now, for a moment, on the perturbations of society, the devices and combinations of parties, and the appliances of corruption, to which the electoral body is at all times exposed. Could these functions be performed with results so generally auspicious, if the people of the United States did not, as a mass, excel other nations in intelligence, as much as in the good fortune of inheriting such extraordinary institutions?

Look at the operation of this system in yet another aspect. Not only the Constitutions of the several States, but even the Constitution of the Union, stands only by the voluntary consent of the People. By physical force, which the Government could not suppress, they could subvert any or all of these Constitutions. Even without force, and acting only by agreement, but in conformity to certain established conditions, they can change or subvert all these Constitutions. There is indeed no restraining power acting upon them, from within or from without. Practically, they do change the Constitutions of the several States once in twenty years. Yet they work such changes generally without commotion, and they have never made one without replacing the Constitution removed by a better one. A few of the States inherited the jurisprudence of the civil law, and all the others the common and statute laws of England. Does any one deny that they have sagaciously retained all the parts of those excellent codes which were essential to order and civil liberty, and have modified others only so far as was required by the changing circumstances of society and the ever-unfolding sentiments of justice and humanity? Let our logical amendments of the rules of evidence, and our simple processes of pleading and practice in courts of justice and our meliorations of imprisonment for debt, and of eleemosynary laws, and of penitentiary systems, vindicate the intellectual vigor and wisdom of the American people.

Modern invention, until the close of the last century, was chiefly employed in discovering new laws of nature, and in shaping those discoveries into the forms of theories and maxims. Thus far, in the present century, Invention has employed itself in applying those theories and maxims, by various devices of mechanism, or otherwise, to practical use. In Europe, those devices are chiefly such as regard esthetic effect. In America, on the other hand, those devices are such as have for their object the increase of power. Required to subdue nature through a broad range quickly, and to bring forth her various resources with haste, and yet having numbers inadequate and capital quite unequal to such labors, the American studies chiefly economy and efficiency. He has examined every instrument, and engine, and combination, and composition, received from his elder trans-atlantic brother, in the light of those objects, and has either improved it, or devised a new and better one. He aims at doing the most that is possible as quickly as possible; and this characteristic is manifested equally in his weapons of war and in his instruments of peace, whether they are to be used in the field, or in the workshop, on the land, or on the sea—the fire-arm, the ax, the plow, the railroad, the clipper-ship, the steam-engine, and the printing-press. His railroads cost less and are less perfect than those in other countries, but he builds ten miles where they have only three. He moves passengers and freights on such roads and in his ships with less safety, but with greater cheapness and velocity. He prepares his newspapers, his magazines, and his treatises, with less care, but he prints a hundred for one. If the European has failed to give him a necessary principle, or to embody it in a practical machine, he finds out the one, or constructs the other promptly for himself. He wanted machines for working up his forests, and he invented the saw-gang, and the grooving and planing machines; for cleaning his cotton, and he invented the gin; for harvesting his wheat, and he invented the reaper. He needed mechanical force to navigate his long rivers and broad lakes, and he converted the steam engine into a marine power. He needed dispatch in communicating intelligence, and he placed his lightning-rod horizontally, and beating it into a wire, converted it into a writing telegraph.

Fifty years ago there was no American Science and no American Literature. Now there is an American tenancy in every intellectual department, and none acknowledge its presence and usefulness more freely than those whose fame has least to fear from competition.

It seems to me that this intellectual development of the United States is due chiefly to the adoption of the great idea of universal emulation. Our constitutions and laws, open every department of human enterprise and ambition to all citizens without respect to birth, or class, or condition, and steadily though cautiously exert a power quite effective in preventing any accidental social inequality from becoming fixed and permanent.

There still remains the question whether the moral development is coördinate with those of physical power and mind in the United States. A republic may be safe, even though it be weak, and though it be in a considerable degree intellectually inactive, as is seen in Switzerland; but a republic cannot exist without virtue.

It will not suffice to examine the question through the lens of traditional prejudice. A kind of reverence is paid by all nations to antiquity. There is no one that does not trace its lineage from the gods, or from those who were especially favored by the gods. Every people has had its age of gold, or Augustan age, or heroic age—an age, alas! forever passed. These prejudices are not altogether unwholesome. Although they produce a conviction of declining virtue, which is unfavorable to generous emulation, yet a People at once ignorant and irreverential would necessarily become licentious. Nevertheless, such prejudices ought to be modified. It is untrue, that in the period of a nation's rise from disorder to refinement, it is not able to continually surpass itself. We see the present plainly, distinctly, with all its coarse outlines, its rough inequalities, its dark blots, and its glaring deformities. We hear all its tumultuous sounds and jarring discords. We see and hear the past, through a distance which reduces all its inequalities to a plane, mellows all its shades into a pleasing hue, and subdues even its hoarsest voices into harmony. In our own case, the prejudice is less erroneous than in most others. The Revolutionary age was truly a heroic one. Its exigencies called forth the genius and the talents and the virtues of society, and they ripened amid the hardships of a long and severe trial. But there were selfishness, and vice, and factions, then, as now, although comparatively subdued and repressed. You have only to consult impartial history, to learn that neither public faith, nor public loyalty, nor private virtue, culminated at that period in our own country,* while a mere glance at the literature, or at the stage, or at the politics, of any European country, in any previous age, reveals the fact that it was marked, more distinctly than the present, by licentious morals and mean ambition.

Reasoning *à priori* again, as we did in another case, it is only just to infer in favor of the United States an improvement of morals from their established progress in knowledge and power; otherwise, the philosophy of society is misunderstood, and we must change all our courses, and henceforth seek safety in imbecility, and virtue in superstition and ignorance.

What shall be the test of the national morals? Shall it be the eccentricity of crimes? Certainly not; for then we must compare the criminal eccentricity of to-day with that of yesterday. The result of the comparison would be only

* "I ought not to object to your reverence for your fathers, as you call them, meaning, I presume, the Government, and those concerned in the direction of public affairs; much less could I be displeased at your numbering me among them. But, to tell you a very great secret, as far as I am capable of comparing the merits of different periods, I have no reason to believe that we were better than you are. We had as many poor creatures and selfish beings in proportion, among us, as you have among you; nor were there then more enlightened men, or in greater number, in proportion, than there are now."—*John Adams's Letter to Josiah Quincy, Feb.* 9, 1811.

this, that the crimes of Society change with changing circumstances.

Loyalty to the State is a public virtue. Was it ever deeper-toned or more universal than it is now? I know there are ebullitions of passion and discontent, sometimes breaking out into disorder and violence; but was faction ever more effectually disarmed and harmless than it is now? There is a loyalty that springs from the affection that we bear to our native soil. This we have as strong as any people. But it is not the soil alone, nor yet the soil beneath our feet and the skies over our heads, that constitute our country. It is its freedom, equality, justice, greatness and glory. Who among us is so low as to be insensible of an interest in them? Four hundred thousand natives of other lands every year voluntarily renounce their own sovereigns, and swear fealty to our own. Who has ever known an American to transfer his allegiance permanently to a foreign power?

The spirit of the laws, in any country, is a true index to the morals of a people, just in proportion to the power they exercise in making them. Who complains, here or elsewhere, that crime or immorality blots our statute-books with licentious enactments?

The character of a country's magistrates, legislators, and captains, chosen by a people, reflect their own. It is true that in the earnest canvassing which so frequently recurring elections require, suspicion often follows the magistrate, and scandal follows in the footsteps of the statesman. Yet, when his course has been finished, what magistrate has left a name tarnished by corruption, or what statesman has left an act or an opinion so erroneous that decent charity cannot excuse, though it may disapprove? What chieftain ever tempered military triumph with so much moderation as he who, when he had placed our standard on the battlements of the capital of Mexico, not only received an offer of supreme authority from the conquered nation, but declined it?

The manners of a nation are the outward form of its inner life. Where is woman held in so chivalrous respect, and where does she deserve that eminence better? Where is property more safe, commercial honor better sustained, or human life more sacred?

Moderation is a virtue in private and in public life. Has not the great increase of private wealth manifested itself chiefly in widening the circle of education and elevating the standard of popular intelligence? With forces which, if combined and directed by ambition, would subjugate this continent at once, we have made only two very short wars —the one confessedly a war of defense, and the other ended by paying for a peace and for a domain already fully conquered.

Where lies the secret of the increase of virtue which has thus been established? I think it will be found in the entire emancipation of the consciences of men from either direct or indirect control by established ecclesiastical or political systems. Religious classes, like political parties, have been left to compete in the great work of moral education, and to entitle themselves to the confidence and affection of society, by the purity of their faith and of their morals.

I am well aware that some, who may be willing to adopt the general conclusions of this argument, will object that it is not altogether sustained by the action of the Government itself, however true it may be that it is sustained by the great action of society. I cannot enter a field where truth is to be sought among the disputations of passion and prejudice. I may say, however, in reply first, that the Governments of the United States, although more perfect than any other, and although they embrace the great ideas of the age more fully than any other, are, nevertheless, like all other Governments, founded on compromises of some abstract truths and of some natural rights.

As Government is impressed by its Constitution, so it must necessarily act. This may suffice to explain the phenomenon complained of. But it is true, also, that no Government ever did altogether act out, purely and for a long period, all the virtues of its original Constitution. Hence it is that we are so well told by Bolingbroke, that every nation must perpetually renew its Constitution or perish. Hence, moreover, it is a great excellence of our system, that sovereignty resides, not in Congress and the President, nor yet in the Governments of the States, but in the people of the United States. If the sovereign be just and firm and uncorrupted, the Governments can always be brought back from any aberrations, and even the Constitutions themselves, if in any degree imperfect, can be amended. This great idea of the sovereignty of the people over their government glimmers in the British system, while it fills our own with a broad and glowing light.

> "Let not your King and Parliament in one,
> Much less apart, mistake themselves for that
> Which is most worthy to be thought upon,
> Nor think they are essentially the STATE.
> Let them not fancy that the authority
> And privileges on them bestowed,
> Confer'd, are to set up a majesty,
> Or a power or a glory of their own;
> But let them know it was for a deeper life
> Which they but represent;
> That there's on earth a yet auguster thing,
> Veil'd though it be, than Parliament or King."

Gentlemen, you are devoted to the pursuit of knowledge in order that you may impart it to the State. What Fenelon was to France, you may be to your country. Before you teach, let me enjoin upon you to study well the capacity and the disposition of the American people. I have tried to prove to you only that while they inherit the imperfections of humanity they are yet youthful, apt, vigorous, and virtuous, and therefore, that they are worthy, and will make noble uses of your best instructions.

www.ingramcontent.com/pod-product-compliance
Lightning Source LLC
LaVergne TN
LVHW011140110826
845150LV00008B/2431
9781418193140